WEDDING ESSENTIALS

WEDDING VIOLIN SOLOS

AUDIO ACCESS INCLUDED

PLAYBACK+
Speed • Pitch • Balance • Loop

To access audio visit:
www.halleonard.com/mylibrary
Enter Code
6961-9912-4937-0855

ISBN 978-1-4234-7689-4

HAL•LEONARD® CORPORATION
7777 W. BLUEMOUND RD. P.O. BOX 13819 MILWAUKEE, WI 53213

Visit Hal Leonard Online at
www.halleonard.com

CAN YOU FEEL THE LOVE TONIGHT

from Walt Disney Pictures' THE LION KING

Music by ELTON JOHN
Lyrics by TIM RICE

GABRIEL'S OBOE
from the Motion Picture THE MISSION

Words and Music by
ENNIO MORRICONE

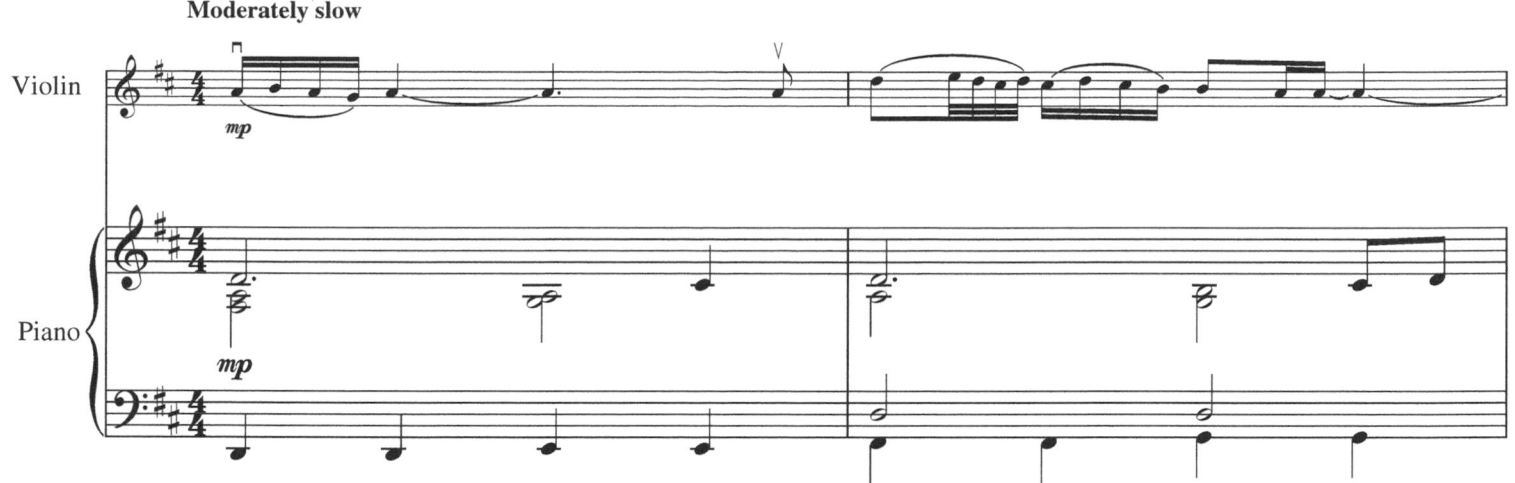

GROW OLD WITH ME

Words and Music by
JOHN LENNON

HERE, THERE AND EVERYWHERE

Words and Music by JOHN LENNON
and PAUL McCARTNEY

HIGHLAND CATHEDRAL

By MICHAEL KORB
and ULRICH ROEVER

I WILL BE HERE

Words and Music by
STEVEN CURTIS CHAPMAN

WEDDING PROCESSIONAL
from THE SOUND OF MUSIC

Lyrics by OSCAR HAMMERSTEIN II
Music by RICHARD RODGERS

To Coda ⊕

For the entrance of the Bride

THE LORD'S PRAYER

By ALBERT H. MALOTTE

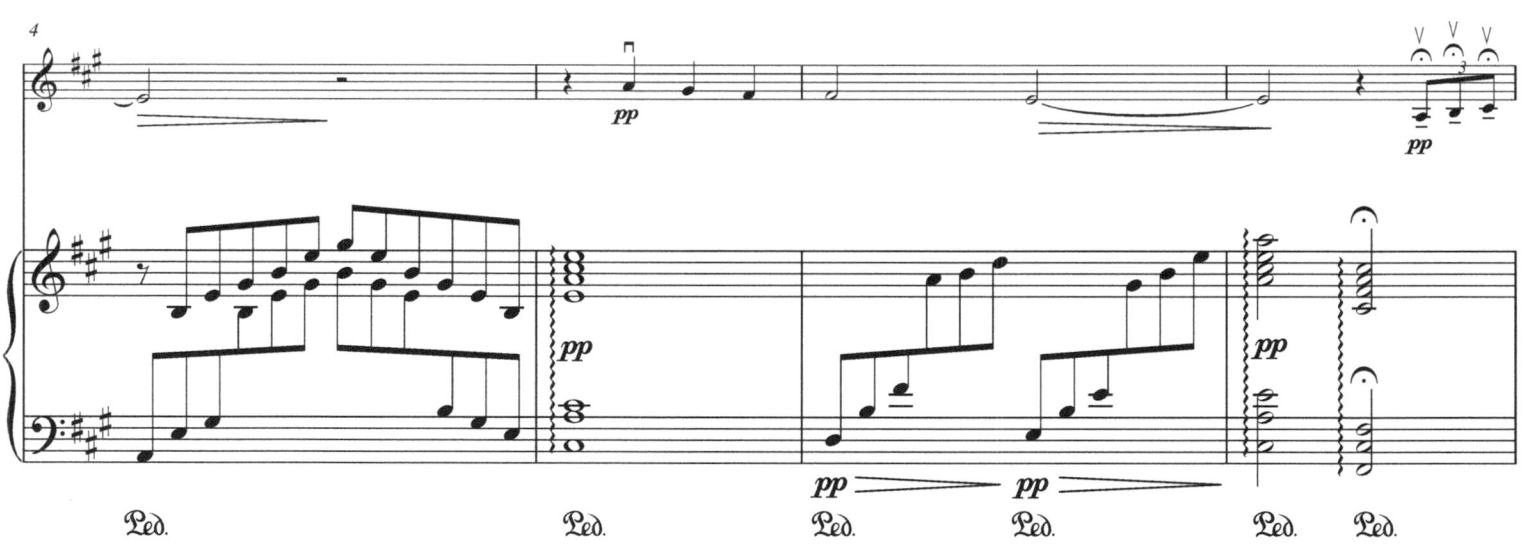

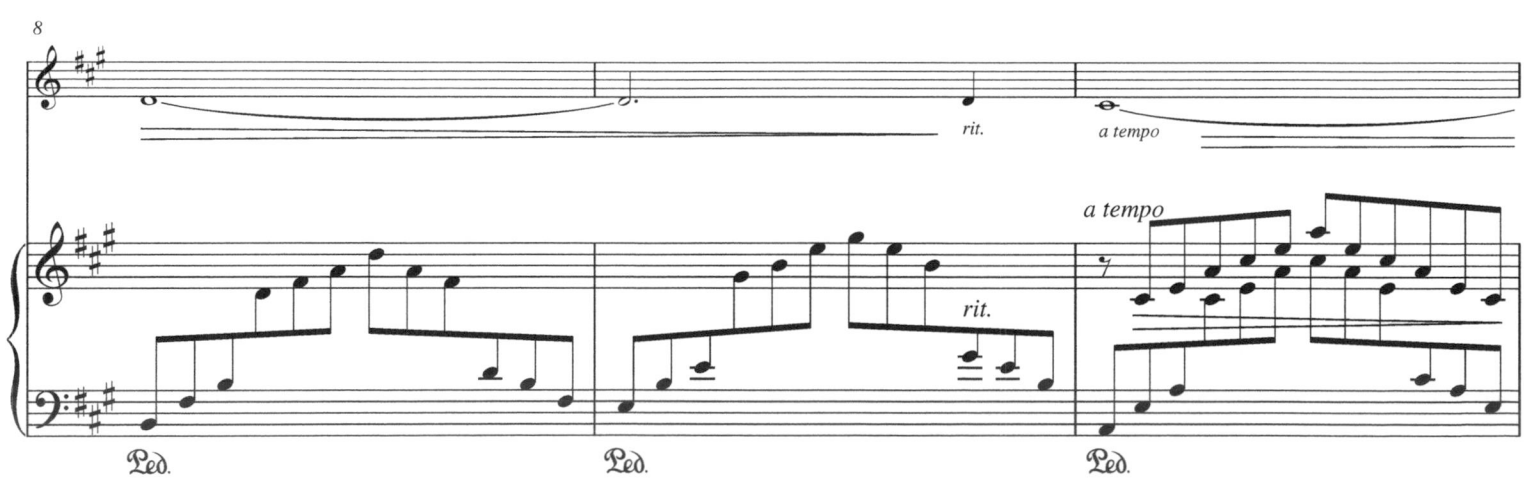

Poco meno mosso, e sonoramente

SUNRISE, SUNSET
from the Musical FIDDLER ON THE ROOF

Words by SHELDON HARNICK
Music by JERRY BOCK

To Coda ⊕

YOU RAISE ME UP

Words and Music by BRENDAN GRAHAM
and ROLF LOVLAND